S0-AGK-009

MAR 2 2 2021

1

Dear Reader –

Can you imagine what America was like 100 years ago? For Olivia, life seemed normal.   She lived in a nice home in a small town in Tulsa, Oklahoma. Her dad owned a department store and her mom was a school teacher. She had a grandmother and four siblings, Irene, Leslie, Samuel 'SD' Jr and Naomi. Her eldest sisters played the piano. Her brother loved to tell jokes. Olivia adored books and enjoyed going to school.   Her family worked hard and lived peacefully.

Olivia's world changed when she woke up one morning, on June 1, 1921. In the story you are about to read, six year-old Olivia's family would never be the same after this day. Many African-Americans were taken from their families, never to return again. Many homes, businesses and churches were set on fire. Olivia quickly learned that these bad things happened to her family because of the color of their skin. Olivia witnessed racism for the first time in her young life. Sadly, many White Americans hated Black Americans because they were very successful business owners, teachers, doctors and lawyers. They were so angry that they destroyed their businesses and homes and made certain they would never be prosperous in Tulsa again.

Sometimes life is not fair. Sometimes life is very scary too. When unfair and scary things happen, you have to be brave. You can decide to help someone who needs help. You can decide not to allow the bad things in life keep you from being your very best. You can decide to win even if everything around you has fallen apart. It's all up to you and this is the lesson Olivia had to learn at a very early age.

Read more, know more…be Inspired!
~S E A

To my three little bravehearts *Savannah, T.J. & Isaac* and their Papa braveheart, *Terry*. To Dr. Olivia J. Hooker, an American Trailblazer and Hero – Thank you for your service to our country and for your outstanding contributions to communities far and wide. I feel honored to be the first to publish your story for young readers; thank you for your blessing.
~S. E. A.

No part of this publication may be reproduced, stored in retrieval system, or transmitted in any form or by any means, electronic, mechanical, photocopying, recording, or otherwise, without written permission of the copyright owner.
ISBN 978-1537610443
Text and illustrations copyright © 2016 by Shameen E. Anthanio-Williams. Author retains full rights of text and illustrations.
Library of Congress Control Number: 2016912976

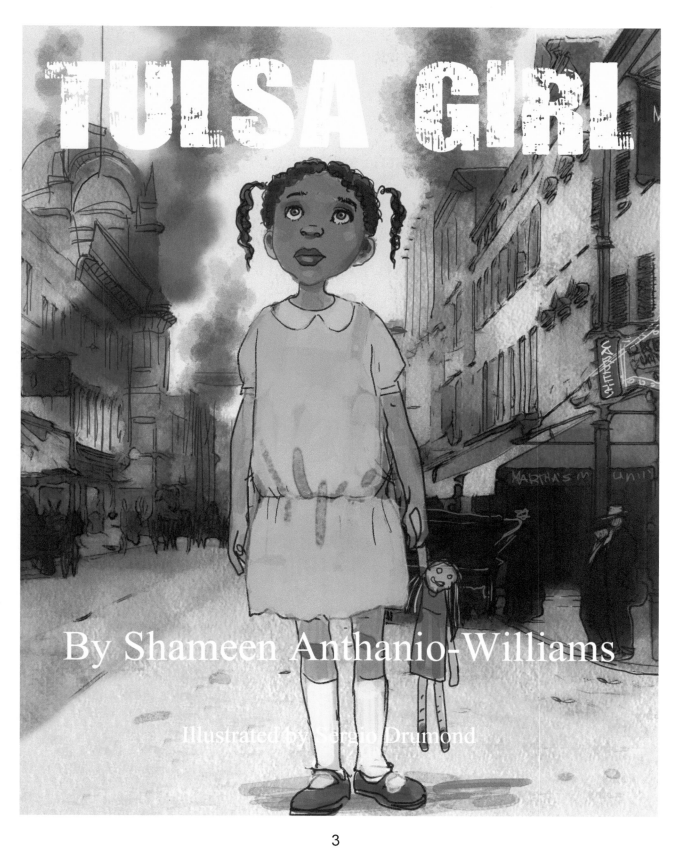

TULSA GIRL

By Shameen Anthanio-Williams

Illustrated by Sergio Drumond

The Tulsa sun warmed the house

She woke up with a smile

Anticipating the school day

Though it hadn't been a while

Olivia Hooker loved to read

And school she loved to do

She was happy for the opportunity

To learn something new

For not so long ago

In this same land of the free

Black boys and girls in America

Weren't allowed to read

But as Olivia readied herself for school

She noticed something odd

While the sun was shining brightly

Roof sounds made her prod:

Mama, why is it hailing

When the sun is stretched so wide?

Her mother turned to face Olivia

And quickly pulled her aside

She motioned her to the window

On a hill stood a gun in plain view

You see it's not hail you hear on the roof top

It's your country shooting at you

With a puzzled heart she judged the gun

Whose flag waved high and new

Didn't she say Pledge of Allegiance

To those same colors in school?

Then at once the door swung open

There stood the first of many

Men with guns and angry faces

Come to take Dad and Sammy

What terrible thing did Daddy do

But own a store and pray?

What bad thing did her brother do

But go to school each day?

By then she hid beneath a table

And watched the angry men

Aren't these our visiting salesmen?

I thought they were our friends?

But today they weren't so friendly

And what they did wasn't right

They tore up all the furniture

They torched everything in sight

But amidst the frightful scene

Her mom was quick to fend

The home she worked so hard to build

She headed for the gunman

Why are you shooting at innocent people?

You know this isn't right!

The gunman ordered her to leave

But she wouldn't without a fight

She handed him the baby

And marched her way back

home

With water buckets she put out fires

Olivia watched her in a zone

Olivia sat underneath the oak table

With the worst fear you could imagine

She didn't know if she'd live or die

As all of this was happening

Though the fires went out and the family rejoined

And the sun yet beamed so bright

Scenes from the massacre stayed in her mind

And kept her up all night

One day the family moved to Kansas

To have a brand new start

They found a nice home and a church

Memories of Tulsa soon far apart

But when it was time to go to school

Olivia wouldn't budge an inch

Mom asked her why she wouldn't go

Olivia replied in stubborn defense:

If the teachers look like the men with torches

Who set my doll clothes aflame

If they smile at me like the ones with axes

Who were mean and heartless just the same

If the teachers look like that angry mob

That took my family away

If the principal looks like the guy with the gun

I'll never go to school, No way!

Olivia's mom knew she had nightmares

But she knew she loved school too

So she decided to find a doctor

To seek help on what to do

The doctor told mom *keep her home*

She'll be bored and beg to go

But that plan didn't work because she loved to read

So each day the answer was still no

Her mom hoped she'd change her mind

So she prayed and prayed and prayed

For school would be her only chance

At being great one day

But each night dark memories of Tulsa

Took her to the most terrible scenes

Until one night something happened

As her mother appeared in her dream

It was the instant her mother charged the gunman

And demanded her rights be recognized

She moved with courage, strength and dignity

Grit bellowed from her eyes

The next day Olivia awoke to a bright new day

But this time with a changed mind

She would not stop going to school

Because of a terrible moment in time

She knew her forefathers sacrificed their lives

For the freedoms they all sought

Hundreds even died during the Tulsa massacre

Over the right to live freely; is why they fought

So her mother found another school

And Olivia's fear had long since waned

She charged ahead to the grand place of learning

With her mother's courage flowing through her veins

CPSIA information can be obtained
at www.ICGtesting.com
Printed in the USA
LVHW071045290121
677650LV00016B/129